Exploring Flowers

by Kristin Sterling

first step nonfiction

Lerner Publications Company · Minneapolis

I see **flowers**.

Parts of a Plant

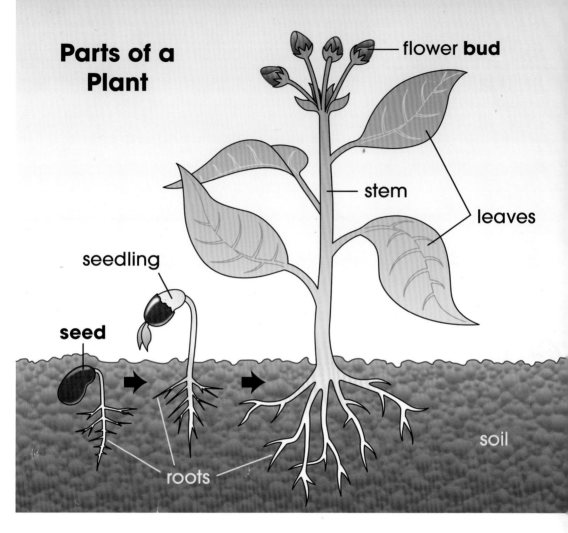

flower **bud**

stem

leaves

seedling

seed

roots

soil

Flowers are parts of plants.

Each plant part has a job.

Fruits, vegetables, and **blossoms** grow from flowers on plants.

Pollen looks like yellow dust.

Pollen makes some seeds
grow into plants.

Pollen is moved by birds and bugs.

Each seed that gets pollen
can become a new plant.

Small buds grow on the
stems of some plants.

Blossoms bloom when buds open.

Flowers on some plants are the first sign of a fruit or a vegetable.

These apples grew from flowers.

Lilacs are pretty flowers that smell good.

People put flowers in their homes.

Flowers are in your home, in the park, and all around you.

Do you see flowers?

All Kinds of Flowers

Red tulips

Blue asters

Small bleeding hearts

Large banana plant

Star-shaped pumpkin plant

Cone-shaped prairie clover

Flower Facts

 Roses are the national flower of the United States.

 Many people buy roses for people they love on Mother's Day and Saint Valentine's Day.

 Flowers smell good. They are used to make perfumes.

 Cherry blossoms are pretty and sweet smelling. Cherries grow from the blossoms.

Did you know olives grow on trees? Trees flower and then olives grow.

 The biggest flower is called the Australian mountain ash.

 The smallest flower is the watermeal plant.

Glossary

 blossoms – a group of flowers

 bud – a small growth on a plant stem that changes into a flower or a leaf

 flowers – the parts of a plant that grow from a stem and make seeds or fruit

 pollen – tiny grains in a flower that look like dust

 seed – a plant part that can make a new plant

Index

The images in this book are used with the permission of: © Astock/CORBIS, p. 2; © Laura Westlund/Independent Picture Service, p. 3; © iStockphoto.com/mammamaart, p. 4; © Smit/Shutterstock Images, p. 5; © Marie C. Fields/Shutterstock Images, pp. 6, 22 (second from bottom); © LilKar/Shutterstock Images, pp. 7, 22 (center); © Mirek Kijewski/Shutterstock Images, p. 8; © Ryan Rodrick Beiler/Shutterstock Images, pp. 9, 22 (bottom); © CoolR/Shutterstock Images, pp. 10, 22 (second from top); © Vasilius/Shutterstock Images, p. 11; © iStockphoto.com/Oleg Prikhodko, pp. 12, 22 (top); © E. Sweet/Shutterstock Images, p. 13; © iStockphoto.com/Linda Kloosterhof, p. 14; © iofoto/Shutterstock Images, p. 15; © Adamsmith/Taxi/Getty Images, p. 16; © cabania/Shutterstock Images, p. 17; © Petr Kratochvil/Shutterstock Images, p. 18 (top); © Alexander M. Omelko/Shutterstock Images, p. 18 (center); © Joy Brown/Shutterstock Images, p. 18 (bottom); © Roman Korotkov/Shutterstock Images, 19 (top); © Richard Peterson/Shutterstock Images, p. 19 (center); © iStockphoto.com/Mark Herreid, p. 19 (bottom). Front cover: © DeshaCAM/Shutterstock Images.

Main body text set in ITC Avant Garde Gothic 21/25. Typeface provided by Adobe Systems.

Lerner Publications Company
A division of Lerner Publishing Group, Inc.
241 First Avenue North
Minneapolis, MN 55401 U.S.A.

Website address: www.lernerbooks.com

Library of Congress Cataloging-in-Publication Data

Sterling, Kristin.
    Exploring flowers / by Kristin Sterling.
        p.   cm. — (First step nonfiction — Let's look at plants)
    Includes index.
    ISBN: 978–0–7613–5779–7 (lib. bdg. : alk. paper)
    1. Flowers—Juvenile literature. 2. Plant anatomy—Juvenile literature. I. Title.
    II. Series: First step nonfiction. Plant parts.
    QK653.S83 2012
    582.13—dc22   2010042986

Manufactured in the United States of America
1 – PC – 7/15/11